Frogs

Carolyn MacLulich

for The Australian Museum

Copyright © 1996 by The Australian Museum.
All rights reserved. Published by Scholastic Inc.
READING DISCOVERY is a trademark of Scholastic Inc.
First published in 1996 by Scholastic Australia Pty Limited.
Printed in Hong Kong.
ISBN 0-590-39069-4

3 4 5 6 7 8 9 10   05 04 03 02 01 00 99

SCHOLASTIC INC.

New York   Toronto   London   Auckland   Sydney

There are thousands of different types of frogs.

Frogs are many sizes and colors.

The Australian tree frog is as big as a hand.

The buzzing frog is as small as a fingernail.

White-lipped frogs are as long as a fork.

Many frogs live in damp places. Some frogs live by creeks and marshes.

Some frogs live in gardens, near taps and ponds.

Some frogs live in trees in rain forests.

Some frogs burrow into damp ground.

Frogs have four fingers on each hand and five toes on each foot. Many frogs have webs of skin between their fingers and toes that help them swim.

Frogs eat insects, spiders and worms. Some frogs eat larger animals, such as lizards, mice or even other frogs.

Male frogs make a croaking sound. They puff up the vocal sac under their chin, which makes the sound louder.

Most female frogs lay eggs in water. The eggs hatch into tadpoles, which don't look like frogs at all.

After a while tadpoles grow arms and legs and lose their tails. Then they are frogs.

Most frogs move about at night and sleep during the day.